The Little Book of
LOVE

Introduction

We are always moved by the sweetest and most mysterious of feelings: Love. The Ancient Greek poetess Sappho tells us in her poems that only Love can give meaning to the actions and lives of people. "*Some say an army of horsemen,/ some of foot soldiers, some of ships,/ is the fairest thing on the black earth,/ but I say it is what one loves.*" Yet, no one can say exactly what Love is. Some feel "butterflies in their stomach," others begin to daydream, their heads in the clouds! Love is always an "as if," an image through which it unfolds. Because it is easier to recognize Love than to explain it in words. So we can only admire it, through images that tell us about it, and through the words that accompany it, and allow ourselves to be struck by Cupid's arrow.

"In our life there is a single color
that gives meaning to both life and art.
It is the color of Love."

- Marc Chagall

"The children lovers are there for no one.
They're elsewhere much further than the night.
Much higher than the day.
In the dazzling light of their first love."

— Jacques Prévert

"You must be tired because you've been running through my mind all day."

– William Shakespeare

"Love begins when
we realize that we've made
yet another mistake."

– Ennio Flaiano

"They're both convinced that
a sudden passion joined them.
Such certainty is beautiful."

- Wisława Szymborska

"A flower is short, but the joy it brings in a minute is one of those things that doesn't have a beginning or an end."

- Paul Claudel

"Things are united by an invisible bond,
you can't pick a flower
without troubling a star."

– Galileo Galilei

"Give me odorous at sunrise
a garden of beautiful flowers
where I can walk undisturbed."

- Walt Whitman

"We went around without looking for each other, but knowing we went around to find each other."

– Julio Cortázar

"He did not say that because
he knew that if you said
a good thing it might not happen."

\- Ernest Hemingway

"All you need is love, love.
Love is all you need."

– The Beatles

"I breathe your breath, and live."

- Sappho

"If there is one thing of which
I am certain, it is that
I want to cover you with kisses."

– Franz Kafka

"Tell me, does your heart sometimes fly away?"

– Charles Baudelaire

"One love One life
When it's one need
In the night."

- U2

"That Love is all there is,
Is all we know of Love."

\- Emily Dickinson

"There are always flowers
for those who want to see them."

- Henri Matisse

"Hold my hand,

take me where time does not exist."

– Hermann Hesse

"If there is no Love, the world is like the wind
that blows outside the window.
You cannot feel it on your hands,
you cannot perceive its smell."

- Haruki Murakami

"The most beautiful sea hasn't been crossed yet.
[...] The most beautiful days we haven't seen yet.
And the most beautiful words I wanted to tell you
I haven't said yet."

– Nazim Hikmet

"I don't make love by kissing,
I make love by dancing."

- Fred Astaire

"Once, pairs of lovers
before separating, would seek out a star,
on which their gazes
could meet at night."

– Christa Wolf

"Give me a thousand kisses,

then a hundred, then another thousand."

– Catullus

"You know, you remind me of a poem
I can't remember, and a song
that may never have existed, and a place
I'm not sure I've ever been to."

- Efraim Medina Reyes

"Great loves are always in movement."

– Alda Merini

"Love is the greatest refreshment in life."

– Pablo Picasso

"Let's love one another quietly,

Thinking that we could, if we wanted,

Exchange kisses and caresses, but that it is worth more to sit next to one another

Listening to the river and watching it run."

– Fernando Pessoa

"When you realize you want to spend the rest of your life with somebody, you want the rest of your life to start as soon as possible."

— Nora Ephron (When Harry Met Sally...)

"Maybe the poets are right.
Maybe Love is the only answer."

- Woody Allen (Hannah and Her Sisters)

"If you are not long,
I will wait for you all my life."

- Oscar Wilde

"Love is a beautiful flower, but we must be brave enough to pick her from the edge of a precipice."

- Stendhal

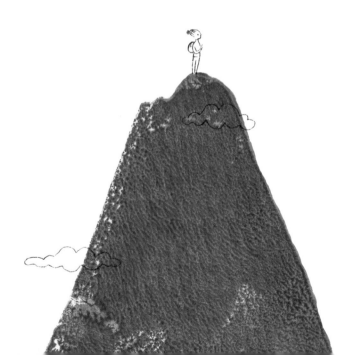

"It's only in the mysterious equation of love
that any logic or reason can be found.
I'm only here tonight because of you.
You are the only reason I am...
you are all my reasons."

— Akiva Goldsman (A Beautiful Mind)

"Love, which exempts no beloved from loving,
took me so strongly with delight in him
that, as you see, it still abandons me not."

– Dante

"Two hearts that love each other like two clocks
are magnetic: what moves in one, the other moves,
because it is only a single pulse which operates
in both, only one force that pervades them."

— Johann Wolfgang von Goethe

"And I'm embracing you without asking anything for fear that it is not true that you live and you love me."

— Pedro Salinas

"Every wave in the sea has a different light,
just like the beauty of those we love."

– Virginia Woolf

ILLUSTRATIONS
Alain Cancilleri (Contextus, Pavia)

INTRODUCTION
Emma Altomare (Contextus, Pavia)

WHITE STAR PUBLISHERS

WS White Star Publishers® is a registered trademark
property of White Star s.r.l.

© 2017 White Star s.r.l.
Piazzale Luigi Cadorna, 6
20123 Milan, Italy
www.whitestar.it

Translation and editing: Contextus Srl, Pavia, Italy
(Louise Bostock)

ISBN 978-88-544-1122-7
1 2 3 4 5 6   21 20 19 18 17

Printed in China